EXTREM POETRY

James Gomez

ISBN 979-8-88851-183-1 (Paperback)
ISBN 979-8-88851-185-5 (Hardcover)
ISBN 979-8-88851-184-8 (Digital)

Covenant Books
11661 Hwy 707
Murrells Inlet, SC 29576
www.covenantbooks.com

To my little angel,
Rachel Marie

INTRODUCTION

Since I can remember, I tend to do everything beyond the limits or not at all! Thus, my imagination and sense of humor (you be the judge).

I've always wanted to compose my poetry into a book and/or music! My love for music is well, to say the least, extreme (go figure)!

So as we embark on this journey together, I hope you enjoy the ride as much as I do.

HISTORY IN THE MAKING

Blink of an eye, came in like a raging storm.
Believe me when I tell you, all were alarmed!

History repeats itself, like the holocaust,
For lack of better words, all were at a loss.

Its name was corona, like that of the beer,
But this one intoxicated us with fear!

They came up with a nickname: COVID-19,
Anything like it, the world had never seen!

People were falling, dropping like flies,
Every day, thousands more would die!

It's still raging like crazy, the world outside,
Cry out to Jesus. In Him, we must confide!

MESMERIZED MEMORY

Under the moonlight, sand between our toes.
Your skin on mine, beneath the heaven's glow!

It's that rolling ocean, that crashing wave,
You make me feel stronger, feel so damn brave.

As the night ushers a new day in.
Take a breath, we'll do it all again!

What a gorgeous sunrise, purple and pink,
You're my life preserve, without you I'd sink!

The sun's rays now making us sweat,
Time spent with you, never forget!

A PSALM OF HUNGER

As a deer pants for water, so my soul pants for Thy Word,
When I humble myself before Thee, I know my prayers are heard!

His Word is perfect, for He is the rock,
Should keep His statutes, and in them I'll take stock!

His royal priest, I try to be,
For in His blood, I was set free!

Never knew how much I'd grieved His heart,
Of His expectations, I fall so short!

In me a clean heart, O God, please create,
With You, shall I tarry. On You, will I wait!

A right spirit within me, won't You renew,
Many are called, but the chosen are few!

Unto me restore, the joy of Thy salvation,
With You I wish to stay, the entire duration!

JUDGE NOT

See through that mirror, deep within your eyes,
You're a lot like me, not so civilized,

It's okay if they don't see us the same,
Just because we're not as easy to tame.

Keep on doing, saying what they will,
Doesn't mean, they're all that better still!

If you don't agree, don't hold a grudge,
Will all meet our Maker. He's the judge!

Though different, deep within, we're all the same,
Comes down, reality. This is no game!

'TIS THE SEASON

This time of year has become too commercialized
Far time, we open our hearts and souls, realize!

Born in a manger, no room at the inn,
He only wants us to change from within!

He died a horrendous death and then He rose,
Did it all for us, obtained inhumane blows!

Yet on the third day, there was an empty cave,
You and I no longer have to be sin's slaves!

He left us His Spirit when He ascended,
Awesomely good and merciful, so splendid!

Don't let this season be just a holiday,
Proclaim His love to others, for this I pray!

ETERNAL EXTREMES

At times, tend to take things to the extreme,
It's not necessarily what I mean.

Perhaps 'cause I live too much in the past,
Don't know, ever-changing world, way too fast!

Gotta slow down, take a deep breath,
Must obtain this before my death!

It's inevitable, all will die,
Pray we will all meet Him in the sky!

And then there will be, finally no past,
For eternity, extreme joy will last!

YOUR DECISION

A beautiful butterfly enhances my vision,
It's then I thank our Father, Holy Ghost, and His dear Son!

Awesomeness of His creation, who could deny,
Only the enemy, he's the father of lies!

And if you allow, it's you he'll deceive,
He'll bring you down, and this you must believe!

Living in a time where we must stand strong,
'Cause telling you, my friends, it won't be long!

Merely a messenger, prophecy will tell,
Read the Word, on the verge of heaven or hell.

MELTING

First gazing at you, began to melt,
The mere sensation from you I felt!

Heart was open, though you had me locked,
My very being, was you who rocked!

Keep rocking me all night long,
Sing you the prettiest love song!

Pray you sing this song in bed at night,
Rescue you, take you off into flight!

And then you too might just melt,
Feel the same way that I felt!

HEAVEN'S CALLING

Wanna go to heaven, not sure I'm ready,
My life's been quite unstable, not so steady.

I tend to live my life out loud,
At times I regret, not so proud!

Thank God that He's merciful, forgives us all.
He's been there for me every time I fall!

Believe me, I've had many a fall,
When these occur, my Father I call!

He's always been there, never let me down,
I love His presence, having Him around.

GOD BLESS AMERICA

One thing's for sure, life's just not fair,
For we've all got our cross to bear!

We'll get plenty of rain, yet a glimpse of sun,
But oh so beautiful when all's said and done!

This land we call home, we're truly blessed,
Though it's slowly becoming a mess!

Need to return, as our Father's foundation,
Back to giving glory to His only Son!

Look what's going on around us, just as He said,
We'll give account of lying in our self-made beds!

CAUTION

Once shook hands with the devil, thought friend of mine,
He's now left this earth, life can be so unkind.

He remained in darkness, that pitch black night,
Instead of choosing Your beckoning light!

Stop and think about it, this ain't no game,
Yet once the cards are dealt, it's hard to tame.

But tame we must do, if indeed we care,
Live among each other, begin to share!

'Cause we're all in this together, can't you see?
It's not about you, it's not all about me!

No, but for real, when it's all said and done,
Every knee will bow and worship the Son!

HARD TO HOLD

Girl, you're just as contagious as a yawn,
Won't you stay with me till the break of dawn?

You make me love you, make me care,
Say you love me too if you dare.

'Cause I'm not easy, that easy to hold,
When created, think He broke the mold!

Yet you could be the one to get me right,
Won't you come over, discuss it tonight?

So is it yes, no, or maybe,
This indecision, driving me crazy.

YOU'RE WELCOME

I met Jesus. I was knocking at His door,
He welcomed me in, and we talked some more.

We spoke of things, my highs and lows,
Informed me what God only knows!

Spite of all I'd done, said He loves me still,
Said go and tell others. This is my will!

Told Him if that's what He wants, that's what
I'll do,
Proclaim His Word to others, wash you brand-new!

And that's why our Father, to us He did send,
Thanks for the welcome, in Jesus's name. *Amen*!

SPIRITUAL SPINACH

Just as spinach was to Popeye,
The Word of God, to you and I!

In Him, there's all power of the extreme,
Cast your cares on Him, and you will be redeemed!

Must look to Him, in all we say and do,
For He created us, can make us new!

It's in Him that we're a new creature,
Remission through His blood, we're made pure!

By no means saying we're of righteousness,
You and I, much more God knows, we're a mess!

Though we're a mess, He loves us in spite,
Only in Him can we be made right!

I CHERISH YOU

Wanna drive you wild, a little insane,
It'll hurt so good, but you'll feel no pain.

Gonna be all right, it will be okay,
Promise I'll make your worries go away!

Cherish your curves, run my fingers through your hair,
If not now, never know just how much I care!

'Cause love and care is about sacrifice,
Wanna touch you softly, make you feel nice!

From the depths, wrote this song, my gift to you.
Maybe someday walk the aisle, say I do!

IT IS WRITTEN

Pray for a mind of holy discretion,
Mind of Christ, Your only begotten Son!

For in doing so, with You, I will rise,
Breaking all barriers, no more disguise!

You came to set the captives free,
As it is written, let it be!

For in You alone, there is life,
No soil untilled, take away all strife!

So, Lord, teach me to teach others what You've shown,
Therefore, throughout the land, Your mercy be known!

LOVE IN ITS PUREST

You came to save sinners, of which I'm the chief,
Yet loved us more, in spite of our unbelief.

Was sent to teach us of a love so pure,
Soften our hearts, give us strength to endure!

More than sufficient is Your grace,
Even when they spit in Your face.

Plucked Your beard, all the hair off Your face,
Then spread Your arms for us to embrace!

When spreading those arms, we nailed You to the cross,
Put in simple terms, we want to be the boss.

Need You as our Savior, can't save ourselves,
Therefore, cease taking Him off the shelf!

PERFECTION

Nobody's perfect, foremost not me,
Frustrating, I try so hard to be!

Seems the harder I try, less I achieve,
This trap also falls in, you must believe.

No matter the fortune, nor the fame,
When comes down to it, we're all the same!

Can put your head, high up in the air,
Knowing you're no better, don't you dare!

There's one that's perfect, Jesus is His name,
Past, present, future, forever the same!

DA-FENCE

Around my heart, had to build this fence,
Was built to keep you away, ever since.

Now you're calling, every now and then,
Emotions can't hang, no, not again.

You put me on, take me off like a shirt,
Can't allow myself again to be hurt.

'Cause that was then, but this is now,
Guess I'll get over you, somehow?

It might be best if we left things alone,
In order to soften my heart of stone.

LIVING TO DIE

When I leave this earth, please don't you mourn, don't dare cry.
Simply means, it was my time to go, time to die!

Come on, face it, comes our day, must all face death,
Lay down, give up the ghost, take our final breath!

This thing called death, I've never been afraid,
It's the afterlife, the choices I made!

Made those choices in my youth, in those wayward days,
Thanks for forgiveness, Lord, were deep uncertain ways!

Wish to enter Your attic, no basement below,
This, my friends, I'm telling you, there don't wanna go!

SHELTER ME

Set out seeking shelter from the storm,
In you, I found refuge, soothingly warm!

You were the one I needed the most,
All my life, had searched coast to coast.

Made me feel new like I wanted to live,
Though both knew, I didn't have much to give.

Came and went, like a raging wind,
All the while, thought you were my friend.

Guess I was just another, all the same,
To me, felt different, but that was in vain!

I'll let you go now, so you can rest,
Deep down, I truly wish you the best!

Feel my heart slowly turning to stone,
Never was good at sleeping alone!

ART IN HEAVEN

Our Father above, we must believe,
Our daily trials, He will relieve!

For we must always trust in Him,
Yes, even when our faith grows dim!

Satan was beautiful, thought he should be boss,
If we follow him, we are destined for loss!

He is only an evil deceiver, here to steal the
souls, of all believers!

In reality, he is merely a liar,
And if we follow him, we are doomed to hellfire!

So let's remain fervent in goodness and prayer,
Because our Father above us truly cares!

TOGETHER WE STAND

I'm a lowlife, or so they think they know,
Think they're better than me, yet does it show?

They make all these laws that contradict,
That keep this nation in dire conflict!

Why can't we learn to live and get along?
Brothers, sisters, let's harmonize this song!

It's our only shot, can't we realize?
Come to our senses, open our eyes!

So come on now, let's all rationalize,
End of this race, we'll be in awe, the prize!

TERMS OF FEAR

Sometimes scared, open eyes, face another day,
At times get scared of living my life this way!

There are times, don't know what to say anymore.
Then there're times, so damn tired of pacing these floors!

Oftentimes, terms of this life, hard to share,
Then again, no one ever said it'd be fair!

Good thing, 'cause I'd swear they were a liar,
Thank God at times for rain, kindle the fire!

They say that fear is merely fear itself,
Choose to take that emotion off my shelf.

PRISONED WITHIN

Feel like a prisoner deep within,
Although I'm out, feels like I'm in.

Try and try to be good, yet still bad,
Often brings tears to my eyes, so sad!

Someday I'll get it right, just wait and see,
Chains will be broken, and then I'll be free!!

The sun will rise, the clouds will part,
It's then, I'll have a brand-new start!!

This old heart of mine has turned to stone,
I'll call our Father, no need of a phone,

No need to press one for English, He'll understand,
For I'm merely me, but He remains the *man*!

SINGER/SONGWRITER

I used to pray more often than now,
Guess I blamed Him, was His fault somehow.

When it all comes down, nobody but me,
Didn't twist my arm, make me eat off that tree.

We'll all face the music, that awesome day,
Go to R & B heaven, this I pray!

Singer/Songwriter, just take a look,
Beginning, finale, wrote the book!

His name is Jesus I'm speaking of,
If let Him in, He'll fill you with love!

YOUR PRESENCE

Absence makes the heart grow fonder, so they say,
Sometimes disagree, only wish you would stay!

'Cause if you'd stay, make you feel brand-new,
For not many have, merely a few.

Gotta work at this, benefits will pay off,
Get you higher, taking you down in the loft!

More than comfort, we could share in the hay,
Not just tonight, but tomorrow all day!

So stay if you will, then won't be absent,
Don't go away, would rather you present!

MY DEAL

Things from me, thought you'd never conceal,
After all, wasn't part of the deal.

Now realize, keening deals just ain't you,
Had never made, if only I knew!

But now I know, never make another,
'Cause you're nothing more than an ex-lover.

I still want for you to have the best,
Do pray you'll find that internal quest!

Yet you never know, just might change still,
Strongly doubt it, wanna make a deal?

WHAT A TRIP

One thing I believe, this life is a trip,
At times not sure, want another sip!

Sometimes this life is hard to swallow,
Makes you feel empty, almost hallow!

Then there are times, couldn't be more sweet,
All must know, trying to be discreet.

Let us recall good times to remain sane,
Following this path, not against the grain!

No round-trip ticket, this one's all we've got,
But can be so beautiful, more than not!

ANCHOR MAKER

You're my anchor in this raging storm,
God only knows, this is the new norm.

'Cause, Lord, like lost sheep, didn't we stray?
Enter again, Your presence I pray!

Seek, ye shall find, knock, it will open,
Blows me away, with me, still coping!

Imagine, Maker of heaven and earth,
Formed me before, still loves me since birth.

What more can I say, what more must I do?
Just gotta proclaim that He loves you too!

THANKFUL

I took a wrong turn down that street,
Found out things there weren't so discreet.

Searched up and down that boulevard,
Saw things there were pretty damn hard!

Gotta roll with the punches, good or bad,
Don't know what got, till realize what had.

Life's not easy, you're sadly mistaken,
Jungle out there, it's life for the taking!

Yet each day's a gift from the heaven's above,
Don't take this for granted, don't you doubt His *love*!

SLEEPING BEAUTY

Can you keep a secret, promise not to tell?
Take you into outer space, ride that carousel.

You've got my mind traveling, the speed of light,
Do you think I could see you, perhaps tonight?

I know you don't know me, nor I you,
But never know, this dream could come true.

Hardly know you, only by name,
Yet feel connected all the same.

Here I go rambling, like it's you I own,
Could we talk about it, pick up the phone!

Might have said too much, guess I'll keep it brief,
I'll dream of you as I drift off to sleep!

MY PRAYER

In my mind, still hear your voice quite often,
Slow down, thinking of you makes me soften.

'Cause sometimes, late at night, wish upon a star,
It's then I say a prayer, wondering where you are

Wonder if ever, you think of me too?
You think it could ever be like brand-new?

Girl, I'd be willing to try if you are,
That wish might just come true, upon that star!

More powerful than that star, almighty prayer,
For deep down within, you know I still care!

RECALLING OUR CONSTITUTION

Times the laws of this land, I don't understand,
Yet politicians still call it a free land.

Thank God, for sure we are indeed free,
Just their definition, different from me.

'Cause freedom's a privilege, comes with a cost,
So don't tell me it's free, mere votes you lost!

Among the greats was Thomas Jefferson,
Back then we weren't divided, we stood as one!

Does this still have an impact, or mere words?
When searching deep within, it seems absurd.

One nation under God, justice, liberty for all,
Check the Word, a nation divided will surely fall!

We're in this together, why must we divide?
When all's said and done, need to stand side by side!

BUILDING CHARACTER

One day, you never know, you might just miss,
Those warm wrapping arms, that sweet wet kiss.

Hope it won't come to that, would be so wrong,
But you never know what you got till it's gone!

If you must go, wanna wish you the best,
Beware of this world will throw extreme test!

What don't kill us makes us stronger,
When stronger, our lives grow longer!

It sometimes seems too long, sometimes not enough,
Builds character within, it'll make us tough!

THE AMERICAN GAME

Started as a game, 'cause we like to play,
It's just not the same, not like yesterday!

Now they've got all these rules, regulations,
Men in zebra suits, don't have the patience!

Already three hours turn into four,
Penalties, commercials, make it last more!

The refs want their time in the limelight.
Remember it's a game, have we lost sight?

This game has become too commercialized,
Like everything else, no real, is this wise?

Money flows fluently, they call it a game,
Think back why you started, don't you feel ashamed?

THE PAST IS NO PRESENT

Past is something, never got over,
Still looking for my four-leaf clover.

Need to quit searching, guess I'll never find,
You're about to drive me out of my mind!

Kinda like the girl of my dreams,
Ain't gonna happen, so it seems.

This heavy load, I seem to carry,
At times, looking back, kinda scary!

Not the first time, I've been scared before,
Gave at the office, then slammed the door!

I keep one foot dangling over the cliff,
No, but wait, mind was altered, went adrift!

THE CHILD IS GRAND

My father once told me many moons ago,
Stay true to yourself, people and things come and go.

Of course, at that time, didn't listen, wish I had,
Instead, chose to be a rebellious, wayward lad!

But now looking back, his words ring so true,
Wish I knew then what I now know, supposed to do!

For this life can lead you, lead you astray,
If allowed, this road will take you the wrong way!

You're too beautiful a child, inside and out,
Don't let anyone tell you different, don't you doubt!

NOT GOOD... BYE

You kissed me goodbye one morning, then left town,
Learning how long it takes, a heart to come down.

Can't you make a U and return?
Or telling me that bridge is burned?

Still feel the pain, you cut me like a knife,
Might as well be dead, for you took my life.

At times awaken, calling your name,
Reach over for you, it's all in vain!

Did you ever love, was it a play?
If so, then why couldn't you stay?

Your love, like the venom of a serpent,
Still feel the poison, ever since you went.

TRANQUILITY

To her, it's merely a repetitive game,
Keeps my life in turmoil, yet love her the same.

Tell myself it's over time and time again,
Hear a knock at the door, guess what, she's back in!

Am I that much a glutton for punishment?
One might think that deranged, hell might be that bent!

This road can only lead to a dead end,
Find myself a different mate, a new friend!

She's out there I know, and someday I'll find,
Then I'll find tranquility, peace of mind!

MY SON

Please don't go where I have gone,
Felt so right, yet was so wrong!

Don't want to do things that I have done,
Please listen carefully, my dear son!

So young and vibrant, seems everything will last,
Yet take it from me, the years fly so fast!

Regret and guilt, are hard to overcome,
Take it from one who knows, my only son!

These heartfelt words are my sincere prayer,
Tell you these things, 'cause I truly care!

MESMERIZED

Gazing at your beauty, can't hardly catch breath,
If you ever leave, of me, would be the death!

See, girl, you've become my habitat,
That's no lie, I'm expressing a fact!

You've got me mesmerized, you blow my mind,
Forever convinced you're one of a kind!

Why did you do this, wonder how?
Guess it doesn't matter anyhow!

I'll love you till the cows come home,
Please don't ever leave me alone!

KARMA

They say what comes around, then goes,
But then again, what do they know?

And just for knowledge's sake, who are they?
How do they know it all, anyway?

They think they do, but have I got news,
Think they're winners, but they also lose!

Guess I'll keep doing what I do,
'Cause don't see what they say is true!

Not always right, too often wrong,
Therefore, I'll go head and end this song.

WELCOME TO THE JUNGLE

It's a jungle out there, you must believe,
Don't be blindfolded, can't be so naive.

Even if scared, can't let them see you shake,
It's then of you, advantage they will take!

There's this deep hole we're all trying to fill,
Some alcohol, others prefer a pill!

Yet when we awaken, there's still this pain,
So when all's said and done, what did we gain?

Don't know all the answers, was asking you,
Staring back at me, like you're asking too!

HOLY TRINITY

The grass below, sweet green melody,
Rising above, brings turmoil you see.

Cause before rising, there must come a fall,
More to the picture, must observe it all.

Being on top isn't always what it seems,
We must humble ourselves and then be redeemed!

So where do we begin, where do we start?
Let's go back, when He created our heart!

We overlook Him, so passively,
Don't forget the Holy Trinity!

FALLEN

I love the way it falls, your gorgeous hair,
Can't you feel my weight, the weight of my stare?

Could gaze at your beauty all day long,
You make my heart sing, that number 1 song!

Find myself thinking of you all the time,
No matter where I turn, you're on my mind!

As long as I live, I'll never forget,
Was that inner fire in my soul you lit!

Mercy, the way you do the things you do,
Guess I'll stop before I continue.

DERAILED

I feel this affair is failing,
Seems that this train is derailing.

Say you love me more than I'll ever know,
Confused, don't know if I should stop or go?

If you really love me, like you say you do,
Why am I so often alone, feeling blue?

I don't know what to think, don't know what to do,
Wish you would enlighten me, only wish I knew!

It's your turn, you're on stage,
Is this the end of the page?

Get the feeling I'm not your kind,
Let me know before I lose my mind.

FOR BETTER OR WORSE

I know things could be a lot worse,
Then again, let me say this first.

Just because at this time, we're so very down,
Doesn't mean these clouds will always be around.

You've seen me at my worst, seen my best,
It's not something I say in jest.

Things will get better if you'd only stay,
If not tomorrow, then maybe today!

Your choice, we all have our free will,
Pray you choose to stay with me still!

GOOD LUCK, GOODBYE

Too damn headstrong, you just won't surrender,
You're nothing more than a mere pretender.

I gave and gave, have nothing more to give,
Hell, you took away my reason to live!

I cherished your every word spoken,
I would have never left you broken!

You took my soul, robbed me of my heart,
I'm just numb, so tell me where to start?

Can't use me anymore, you took it all,
What comes around, goes around, you'll have your fall.

THE BATTLE WITHIN

These demons inside, residing still.
One would think by now, they'd had their fill,

But it's another day, another dollar lost,
And again tonight, I'll look back and count the cost.

Met my criteria this very day?
Did leave a mark, say what I had to say?

Was there a purpose, indeed was I sent?
When looking within, did I find content?

So where do I go? Where haven't I been,
When all's said and done, here I go again.

AN ANGEL BEYOND

How can this loser ever win, God knows I try,
No avail, but I'll keep on till the day I die,

Think of heaven, you're the first that crosses my mind,
You're the most beautiful angel, I'll ever find!

Knew what He was doing, when formed you in His hands,
And that's why He's the boss, yea that's why He's the man!

When you gaze into a mirror, how could you forget,
Epitome of gorgeousness is what you reflect!

If you gave me the time of day, it would blow my mind,
Because another on this earth, I could never find!

REASONING

Though once upon a time, I was so naive,
Was stepped on, let out, but now I believe.

Believe had to go through what I went through,
Made me what I am today, made brand-new!

Nevertheless, have lots of squeaks, more pain,
Seen many sunny days, yet share of rain!

Thankful to have been, when all's said and done,
Not on my behalf, owe all to His Son!

Reason for the season, know you've heard,
Anything shy is simply absurd!

REMEMBER WHEN

These rivers keep flowing through my mind,
Searching yesterday, I still can't find.

Guess have to admit, she's gone forever,
Those days I presume, will be never.

She was so sweet way back when,
Yet this is now, that was then.

It seems like yesterday, things were so right,
In the blink of an eye, changed overnight.

Almost scared to awaken a new day,
But time will tell, or that's what they say.

ALL THAT

Girl, you make my life full, so complete,
In your loving arms, I feel the heat.

At times, I'm right yet more often wrong,
Count on this, will love you all life long!

You bring me joy, then fill me with pain,
You are my sunshine, you are my rain!

Trying to say you're my everything,
Make my heart smile, you make me sing!

For it's when I'm broke, you mend,
And that's why you're my best friend!

WEAK ENDS

Fridays aren't too good, in fact they're kind of sad,
That's the day she left me, took all I had!

Saturdays, all I do is moan,
I'll never make it all alone.

Sunday mornings, in church I pray,
Dear, Lord, why did she go away?

Send me another, won't You please?
Growing tired, begging on my knees!

But You're the boss, You're the man,
Was this a part of Your plan?

Can't figure, for the life of me,
Guess I oughta just let it be.

STAR WRITTEN

I believe we were written in the stars,
If you'll be my Venus, I'll be your Mars!

Wish you didn't have to go away,
Won't you change your mind and choose to stay?

Worth your while, I'll treat you like royalty,
If this you don't believe, just wait and see!

Wanna touch every pore, your very soul,
I'll make you feel complete, make you feel whole!

So what do you say, my heart's on the line,
Wish you'd consider staying, be all mine!

NO DENYING

Call me bad company, that's what they say,
Not so much choice, just seems to go that way.

I've tried and tried to clean up my act,
Might not believe it, but it's a fact!

Persistently trying, all day and night,
Guess you might say, I just can't get it right!

An *E* for effort, indeed this much I've claimed,
When they lay me to rest, won't forget my name!

You might think it's easy, being so bad,
To tell you the truth, it's really quite sad.

But wait, I'm not asking for sympathy,
Except from the Lord, I'm on bended knee!

LORD KNOWS

I can't eat, define that word called sleep,
Damn it, girl, you got me in far too deep!

Since I met you, think I've lost my mind,
Been searching everywhere, still can't find!

Just how do you get me so mesmerized?
In spite of all of your seductive lies!

Are you that good, or am I that naive?
Hope it's the prior, would like to believe.

Could be wrong, Lord knows wouldn't be the first,
With you, I'm not sure if I'm blessed or cursed.

HUMANITIES' CLOSURE

No one's got time for others anymore,
Like those good old days we shared back before.

Before technology took over,
Then lost sight of our four-leaf clover.

We're no longer human, we're robots,
Think we'll make it like this, I think not!

My strong opinion, none of us know,
On stage, trying to put on a show!

But every show must come to an end,
That's no illusion, the mere truth, my friend.

HURT SO GOOD

If I never met you, I wouldn't have felt the pain,
Looking back, for sure it left a stain.

Yet the pain turned into quite a dance,
That dance led to the most gorgeous romance!

Romance that made me what I am today,
I'm so glad with me, you chose to stay!

Gave me a purpose, reason to go on,
Therefore, I'll love you till the break of dawn!

A new day, 'tis the morning dew,
I open my eyes, loving you!

BEFORE

Really don't understand this world anymore,
I used to think so, but that was before.

Before epidemics and murders galore,
I see things so different, different from before!

Will we ever get back, I just don't see,
Less we come together in harmony!

Don't see happening, too much division,
Come together, make a strong decision!

When it comes down to it, we must decide,
How about trust Jesus being our guide!

SKIN DEEP

What cha think happen, if we all showed skin?
Cause though different, all same deep within.

So let us bond, one with each other,
We've got this one life, not another!

We're all His children, God's family,
Think He wants it this way, no indeed!

Show our true colors, without any doubt,
Perhaps we just might find a way out.

This childish fighting tears us apart,
Let's erase the board, make a new start!

HEAVENLY SKY

'Tis purple and pink, God's heavenly sky,
Why do we complain, still ask myself why?

Because we've been blessed more times than most,
Him, not us, our Superior Host!

So let's give credit where credit's due,
It's not about me, not about you.

We owe Him all the honor, all glory,
For it's all about Him, it's His story!

Face the facts. Mankind, what have we done?
Can we get real, it's our Father's Son!

THIS TOO WILL PASS

At first you had me, tattered and torn,
Seems things used to wear so well, are worn.

Like the day you left me all alone,
Wouldn't hear, if called me on the phone!

Like another ship leaving harbor,
In spite of all I did to win her!

My father used to say, "This too will pass,"
Though at the moment, cuts like jaded glass!

Comes around, goes around, this too you'll find,
Don't mean to be so blunt, so damn unkind!

EQUALITY

Equal we were born, equal we should stay,
Forget tomorrow, I'm talking today!

When Christ bore our sins, it wasn't just for you and me,
Did it to save us all from iniquity!

Open your mind, then look deep within,
You're not much different from her or him!

Separate cultures, religions, or race,
Come together, repent, do an about-face!

Equal we're created, equal we must stay,
This will be required of us on Judgment Day!

BEFORE THEN AFTER

There's no rainbow before the rain,
Joy in the morn, after night's pain.

It seems there's only glory,
At the end of the story.

Must keep seeking till we reach the end,
To realize what it's about, my friend!

All have a purpose sent from way up high,
Must find it, then live it, before we die!

Brothers and sisters, let's join in prayer,
Not until then will we show true care!

TROUBLED WATER

I was born down there, down by the river,
Thoughts come back at times, they make me shiver.

It's like a bridge over troubled water,
But I'll get back up, no time to falter.

'Cause time is all we've got, doesn't last long,
Trying to portray the words in this song!

Gotta stand up and sing it out loud,
All got skeletons, keep walking proud!

Yea, all got things that we regret,
But can't give up, ain't over yet!

That fat lady singing, I never heard,
That's my story, I'm sticking to my word!

IMAGINE THAT

If tomorrow never came, only today,
Would you do the same things, act the same way?

Sometimes wonder if we might just make a change?
No really, think about it, might rearrange.

Imagine for real if this were our last,
Would you live today like yesterday's past?

Me, myself, probably change my mind,
Catch glimpse of a future, might just find!

If there's a tomorrow, want you there,
Bowing heads tonight, this is my prayer!

BITTERSWEET

Have been with this girl now for forty-two years,
She's caused me much anguish and plenty of tears!

In the beginning, so cunning with seduction,
But now looking back, was all a game, just for fun.

She led me into superficial happiness,
Not caring that my life was becoming a mess.

Had me searching like a vagabond,
Of her luring ways, I grew so fond!

This woman's name, we'll just call her alcohol,
Don't let her in your life, or you're bound to fall!

FRIENDS FOREVER

Never was much good at long goodbyes,
Always seem to bring tears to my eyes.

For now, say we'll see each other again,
I'm not sure how, I can't even quote when.

Just know you're forever in my heart,
Knew the second we met, from the start!

Dear to my soul, my thoughts are pure,
You're always near, of this be sure!

So for now, let's just leave it at *so long*,
Sincerely sorry if ever did wrong.

MISSING SHIP

You'll sure be one, that's hard to put down,
Already miss not having you around!

Chose to go your way and left me all mine,
When all's said and done, hope you're doing fine!

Me, oh my, not doing so well,
But then again, I'll never tell.

I hope you found what you were looking for,
I wish you the best, for you deserve more!

Guess that was that, and this is this,
Suppose again, my ship I missed!

SENTIMENTAL FOOL

Why must I be so damn sentimental?
Don't forget, add emphasis to mental.

That's why I get stomped on over and over,
Dog returns to its vomit, call me Rover!

Leave me again, and that will be enough,
That was this puppy you heard said, "*Ruf, ruf!*"

Leaving tonight to howl at the moon,
Probably not, but might see you soon,

See you when I see you, your sentimental fool,
'Cause just the mere thought of you still makes me drool.

STRAIGHT UP

This empty bed, a living nightmare,
So glad you chose to show all this care!

Without all this love and care, where would I be?
Drowning in this bottle, bottomless sea!

If that ain't love, hell, I'll give it up,
On your way out, pour me a strong cup!

I don't want it diluted, don't need a mix,
Getting over you is gonna take a strong fix!

Hope you never feel that void, extreme loss,
What comes around goes around, count the cost.

ANSWERED PRAYER

On one hand so beautiful, the other sorrow,
Can't we ride this storm, girl, least until tomorrow?

You're like a meadow, growing in my mind,
Another like you, I'm sure not to find,

Believe me when I say, I have looked near and far,
Spent many lonely nights wishing on a star!

Searched so long for that pot at the end of the bow,
And you were there all along, guess you never know.

Want to thank you, girl, and thank the Lord above,
For sending me this gorgeous angel to love!

GOLDEN RULE

Why was I chosen to sing the blues?
Perhaps it's the rhythm, if you knew,

Don't you know, R & B founded rock?
Sitting on this bay, here on the dock!

I'll sit here forever, so it seems,
'Cause I'm a dreamer, and that's my dream!

My dream is we all come together,
'Spite of race, culture, or whatever!

Why can't we all learn to get along,
What I'm trying to portray in this song!

MY ONE DESIRE

One day for sure, this damn's bound to break,
Hope it's not soon, for heaven's sake.

'Cause we've been through too much, to just let go,
In your heart of hearts, you also know!

Can't we rekindle that burning fire?
Knowing still you're my only desire!

To me, you're the epitome of love,
Synonymously, two hands in one glove!

That's the way it was back then, yesterday,
Only pray through it all, you choose to stay!

RESTLESS

We're restless, it's our instinct,
It's okay, makes us distinct.

Wanna be your platinum silver lining,
Don't leave me here lonely, leave me whining.

'Cause if you left, I have nowhere to go,
In your heart of hearts, this you must know.

It's me for you and you for me,
Two in one, we'll set ourselves free!

What do you say, girl, can we coincide?
Let's not look back and merely say we tried!

LETTING GO

I just can't see, telling you goodbye,
Without you, guess I might as well die.

So in love with you, truly wish the best,
My life, don't know what I'll do with the rest(?)

Sometimes wonder what you'll say when I'm gone,
Will it really matter, what's done is done!

Hope you think of me every now and then,
Back in the good ole days, remember when.

Never forget you, I think of you every day.
Guess I'll let you go, don't know what else to say.

AGAIN

Found myself rolling dice with the devil,
Had stooped so low, was then on his level.

Upon realizing, I fell to my knees,
Relying on God's mercy to save me please!

Believe it or not, He did it again,
Came down from heaven and took all my sin!

Not only me, but if you will allow,
He will take yours also here and now!

For He's the King, He can do it all,
Go to Him, or you're bound to fall.

Just humble yourself, go to Him and ask,
Might be labor to you, to Him it's no task!

SUDDEN REALIZATION

If you would choose to leave me at the break of dawn,
Would have to suck it up and proceed to go on.

Of course, much prefer if you chose to stay,
Sweetheart, would you give me just one more day?

Must say your leaving took me by surprise,
Until then, didn't fully realize!

Now I awaken to an empty bed,
Would much prefer to have you here instead!

Perhaps you could give just one more chance,
Icing on top, I would coat romance!

YOU BELONG

I hear you've been asking how I was,
Well, I guess I'll make it, just because.

Why would you ask, one might think you care,
How could you leave, it just wasn't fair!

I wasn't always easy to be around,
Yet I still miss that beautiful voice, that sweet sound!

I often wonder how you're doing too,
Doing with another the things you do.

Girl, I'm trying to say, I know I was wrong,
But I still want you back where you belong!

HAPPY FATHER'S DAY

A story I wish to tell of a man,
In his shoes, I only wish I could stand.

Consist of pride, ambition, character, and more,
With each passing day, I see more than before.

This man I'm speaking, if you only knew of,
With determination, did it all for love!

Gave me chances when there was no way,
And that is why I'm so proud to say:

I love you. Dad, and I wish you a very blessed Father's Day!

COASTAL STORM

I'd love for you to accompany me,
'Neath the moonlit reflection of the sea.

The rocking waves swaying us to sleep,
Could stay afloat, but let's go deep!

Water's cool, and the stars are warm,
No need for you to be alarmed.

For storms will come, and they will go,
Through them all, be there, you must know!

When and if, we make it to the coast,
You'll know by then, I loved you the most!

Sun's on the horizon, brand-new day,
Asking, darling, to stay for always!

THE RAINBOW

Through this bow I've chased, am still not sold,
Been to the end, still no pot of gold.

Experienced blizzards, cold, and rain,
Deep within the eye remains the pain!

Yet pain, just another four-letter word,
Kinda like life, isn't that absurd?

It is what we make it, or so they say,
Maybe tomorrow, don't think so today!

Awoke, witnessed a beautiful rainbow,
His mercy is new each morn, don't cha know!

ON MY MIND

Still searching, I'm still trying to find,
Ever since you left me, you remain on my mind.

I've searched over here, I've searched then and there,
Just can't seem to find you, not anywhere!

I know you're here, way down deep in my soul,
'Cause, sweetheart, you're that song, sweet rock and roll!

You sing those high notes, so high, then so low,
Gorgeous melody, you and I, we'll know.

You will always hold that place in my mind,
Can't quite figure you out, you're just my kind!

LOVE STRUCK

At first, your love struck me like a bolt of lightning,
To be perfectly honest, it was quite frightening.

Now that I've come to know you, I couldn't ask for more,
For it's you and only you, I've grown to adore!

You're like no other, I've ever known before,
Beautiful sunrise, you and I on a shore!

Wanna cuddle with you forever and always,
Pray you'll bless me with your presence all our days!

Steam descending from your body, my desire,
Like an out-of-control forest-blazing fire!

You've had a hold on me, girl, from the very start,
You will always have that special place in my heart!

3 MAKES 2

3 makes 2, yes, it sounds absurd,
Yet firmly stated in His Word.

For He created us, male and female,
After our fall, sent His Son to make bail!

Must always remember, He bailed us out,
In His salvation, we should never doubt!

Comes down to it, there is no other,
Stick closer to you than a brother!

So just like 3 made 2, He's 3 in 1,
He's the Father, Holy Spirit, and Son!

LANDED

Seagull flies overhead, searching for a place to land,
It's like that of an hourglass, the sprinkling sand.

All I ever wanted, I found in you,
Like that of an early, spring morning dew!

Every morning, thank the good Lord above,
For sending me you, my princess to love!

Now that I've found you, feel so complete,
There's no more secrets, can be discreet!

Seagull has landed, just open your eyes,
It's me, sweetheart, wearing no disguise!

IN HIS EYES

In His eyes, I find forgiveness,
Though my life has been, one big mess!

If it weren't for His grace, Lord knows where I'd be,
Each new dawn, look around, and it's all I see!

Pray everyone would stop, take a deep breath,
In Him, you'd find there's life, opposed to death!

In His eyes, for us He only wants the best,
In Him only, you'll find complete peace and rest!

In the mirror, wanna see myself in His eyes,
Then I'll find true knowledge, I will see myself as wise!

LONGING FOR YESTERDAY

Yesterday, I always thought she'd be here to stay,
But there I went thinking, up and flew away.

I often long for her to come back,
Like that old song, she hit the road, Jack.

It felt so right, but I guess I was wrong,
Now I continually sing blue songs!

This time, never know? I might just learn,
Only wish, every day she would return!

I gotta face the facts, realize it's over,
Still out here searching for my four-leaf clover.

THE GIFT

As I awoke this morning, opened my eyes,
It was then and there, I finally realized!

Each new day is a gift, from the King on high,
Because without this gift, we would surely die!

Not only die, but eternal torment,
Instead gifted us with His Son, He sent!

Sent to die a horrific, inhumane death,
Third day gave His Son, this same gift of breath!

Our turn to return the gift, surrender our will,
In spite of our sins and shortcomings, loves us still!

BACK TO ME

Since you left me baby, I got so bored,
Although I've got money, still feel so poor!

So what per tell, am I supposed to do?
How do I continue life without you?

Trying to be logical brings much pain,
Without you here beside me, all is vain!

Won't you please, sweetheart, come back to me?
'Cause you're my honey, and I'm your bee!

Hope to hear from you, like really soon,
If not, I'll write an R & B tune!

WITHOUT A SONG

Without a song, you can't right a wrong,
Without a song, endless days, nights too long.

Without a song, so much I would have missed,
Without a song, void would be thing I wished.

Without a song, couldn't have felt your outstretched hand,
Without a song, through the rain, put me back to dryland!

Without a song, searched for true love, all my life long,
Our Father's Son, might have missed Him without a song!

HAPPY VALENTINE'S DAY

Happy Valentine's Day to you, my love,
Get me so high, I could soar like a dove.

Not a cannibal, but I could eat you up,
There's more where that came from, if that's not enough!

There's not another that can compare,
I pray you feel the same, need your care!

Love you from this day and forevermore,
For it's only you, babe, whom I adore!

I'll love you for all my life,
Hope you still choose to be my wife!

MUSIC IS HER NAME

I like it fast, those screeching cars,
That high-pitched tone of sweet guitars.

Kinda like making love to my ear,
Listen carefully, you too will hear.

Like nothing else, you've ever experienced,
Music will take you places you've never sensed!

Grab a seat, fetch the control, then press play,
Then just kick back and enjoy the new day!

No other luxury, bring you higher,
If allowed, will set your soul on fire!

It's where I tend to find serenity,
From deep within, it's the music in me!

THE GAME

What tomorrow holds only God can tell,
In the meanwhile, life's a carousel.

An amusement park, kinda up and down,
I've searched for answer yet still haven't found.

But I'll keep on searching until I find,
Or perhaps before then, might lose my mind!

It's like that game called Marco Polo,
Hell, I quit, tired of flying solo!

Yet the game goes on, or so they say,
Then again, who are they anyway?

FIGHT THE FIGHT

I long to tenderly kiss your lips,
For it's then that I go on a trip!

Bathroom window in she came, shielded silver spoon,
Then she was off to the races, off to the moon!

Coming back to earth is hard, the hardest part,
We're a lot better off if we just don't start!

'Cause this is all we get, only sure thing,
God only knows what tomorrow may bring!

This horrific storm, pray we make it through,
Don't quit the fight, do the best you can do!

HIGH TIDE

Left me here, all by myself in the cold,
Okay, my bad, ain't like wasn't foretold.

But still, how could you leave me all alone?
Can't seem to face this life all on my own!

I need to know that you will be there,
Need your warm, loving arms, show you care!

I really want to know, is this meant to be?
Or is this another high tide in the sea?

Childish games, I'm getting too old,
I can't be bought, I won't be sold!

IN HONOR

Out there, laying their lives down every day,
While we passively, freely, go our way.

They come back confused, in dire need of care,
We show no sympathy, it's just not fair!

Wait, how can we be so fricking cold,
'Cause of them that we walk streets of gold!

Speaking for myself, we ought to be ashamed,
This is not normal, total insane!

Every time I see one, I salute,
Don't be nonchalant, don't remain mute!

Open your eyes, hell, you might just see,
If not for them, we wouldn't be free!

CEASE-FIRE

Never win, bucking the system little girl,
You must believe, for I've tried, take it from me.

Know how you feel, it's in your genes,
Though right, you're still wrong, so it seems!

Extremely hard at times, to fight the fight,
Something must do, if we believe we're right!

Yet don't forget to think before you leap,
At times, we can get ourselves in too deep!

Then again, He wants us to live in peace,
So therefore, all this fighting must cease!

FOREVER FRIENDS

Just talking with you brings me closure,
True friendship, God knows, trying to be pure.

You make it hard sometimes, 'cause here I go,
Sorry I feel this way, yet still don't know?

Respect your feelings, truly I do,
Only wish you felt the same way too!

But that's okay, gonna be all right,
Sleep alone here, here again tonight.

So, babe, on your pillow, saying your prayers,
Won't you say one for me, wish I were there!

YOUR CALL

So what are you doing for the rest of your life?
Would make me so happy if you'd be my wife!

If you knew the depths of my love for you,
You might just surrender and say I do!

Stop fighting it, girlfriend, simply give in,
I'm at your beckoning call, just say when.

I'd treat you like the princess that you are,
You're my everything, my shining star!

I'm not asking for much, just want it all,
So you know my prayers, you must make that call.

TRUST AND BELIEVE

To some bizarre, others somewhat absurd,
Don't base your opinions, on things you heard.

'Cause people gonna talk, for good or for bad,
Be true to yourself, don't let them make you sad!

A finger pointing, means three pointing back,
That's when you bow up, tell 'em, "Hit the road, Jack!"

Believe in yourself when no one else does,
It's what you gotta do, just because!

Trust in yourself no matter the cost,
If not, you'll only find yourself lost!

INEVITABLE AGE

It seems I've been a prisoner all my life,
God knows, cuts deeper than any two-edged knife!

Long as remember, been confined within,
Self-inflicted suppose, but then again.

We make our beds, then it's there that we lie,
Can't go out like this, not ready to die!

I'm nowhere as young, now that I'm older,
Come on, let's get real, for sure no bolder.

They tell me it's this thing called old age,
They must be old themselves, turn the page.

SOULMATE

If your love, you don't send soon to me,
For sure, girl, it will be the end of me.

'Cause it's you and only you, of this I'm sure,
Damn it, babe, you're so innocent, so damn pure!

Way you do those things, got me out of control,
You've taken my heart, you stole my very soul!

Pray you don't go, leave me all alone,
My soulmate, I'm convinced you're my clone!

Ball's in your court, where do we go from here?
Hope we coincide, let me know, my dear.

THE PROPOSAL

If you'd only walk with me awhile,
Bet I could get you, get you to smile.

'Cause you're the reason, this smile on my face,
There's no one else who could ever replace.

Have mercy, don't turn this smile upside down,
For if you did, in my tears I would drown!

You're my epitome, that sweet song,
Wanna dance with you all my life long!

So on bended knee, if you'll take my hand,
Unbelievable encore will be grand!

Be like the Grand Ole Opry,
Don't believe, just wait and see!

FORGIVE THOSE

For times I've hurt you, I apologize,
When I do this, I just don't realize.

Never get over you, locked in my heart,
Knew this from day one, from the very start!

Never cease to amaze me, blows me away,
On a stormy day, you bring sunshine my way!

For you, I want happiness in all that you do,
Only wish my love was one of those things, so true.

I love you, baby, this much you know,
Guess I'll end this thing and let you go.

SEEK AND YE SHALL FIND

Searching for answers, since once was conceived,
Seeking something in which I can believe.

Out there somewhere, perhaps horizon sun,
Just maybe, His only begotten Son!

Seek long enough, you're sure bound to find,
He'll replenish both your heart and mind!

Well, what do you know, my search is over,
At last, I've found my four-leaf clover!

After all this time that I've spent in vain,
He was there the whole while to take my pain.

OPEN-AND-SHUT CASE

Ironic, most are born in bed,
And there, we'll return, when we're dead.

This life's weird, guess death is more strange,
Pray before then, I make abrupt change!

Lord, help me, for You and I know can't do it alone,
That's why I'm calling from this long-distance telephone!

So glad Your calls aren't being charged,
Plenty to discuss, bill would be large!

You're so loving and filled with grace,
I love You also, rest my case!

FATHER'S DESIRE

Here goes this writer picking up his pen,
Scares me at times, no, that was back then.

Edit, publish, be your paperback writer,
Now I'm strictly a lover, no longer a fighter.

'Cause for real, fighting don't make much sense,
Learn to love one another, straddle that fence!

We're formed from His Hands, there He created,
Deep within my soul, I stand elated!

Help me to fulfill Your desire,
Set my soul on a zealous fire!

YOUR PUPPET

Escape in my music, flee from life,
'Cause this thing cuts sharper than a knife.

The way the sun glistens, off your hair,
Tell me what else can I do, but stare?

This life, sure looks good on you,
Your puppet, tell me what to do!

Wanna make this work out, just right,
Last forever, this very night!

It's a new day, bless God, open my eyes,
You're the first sight I see, I'm mesmerized!

Say you'll stay with me for always,
Through those endless nights, countless days!

To me, you give the ultimate pleasure,
In this life, it's the main thing I treasure!

Must have come from the heaven's above,
'Cause God knows, you ain't nothing but love!

Things you say and the way you do,
You make this old man feel brand-new!

LONESOME ROAD

Pour me a strong one, Mr. Bartender,
It's her love, trying not to remember.

That face, hair, bod, and luscious lips,
Close as I'll get, to heaven's sip.

Got my head spinning round, so twisted,
I recall, it was you I insisted.

Or perhaps, it just could have been me,
More times than often, my worst enemy.

'Cause it gets lonely, this street I walk,
Saying that for real, not merely talk!

MATERIAL THINGS

In the things I used to find treasure, I find no more,
This thing called aging, everything's a chore!

I used to love to take a nice hot shower,
Now have to convince myself, find the power.

Coffee on the porch, God's beauty, the sky,
Still so discontent, I ask myself why?

'Cause I've got more than could ever ask for,
Yet still I find myself wanting for more!

Must come to a time, say enough's enough,
Reality being, it's only stuff.

WAIT A MINUTE

To put off things, in this I've learned to wait,
Call it what you will, it's called procrastinate.

Convincing myself, it can wait till tomorrow,
Knowing all along, piling up brings sorrow.

If practice these habits, will become quite good,
Put off today till tomorrow, think I could?

All comes down to getting things done,
When will I see I've lost, not won?

So that's my story on procrastination,
Like Larry, the cable guy, says, "Get ur done!"

NUMBER ONE

It's what you do when you take my hand,
For it's then I fully understand.

Been places with you never knew exist,
When you give me that look, just can't resist!

For anyone else, never felt this strong,
Deep within my heart is where you belong!

You've been the one I've always dreamed,
Never find you, or so it seemed!

You and I as one, all eternity,
So get on board and fly away with me!

WHAT IF

Take you to paradise, then through the storms,
Make you feel secure in my loving arms!

Wanna take you higher than you've ever seen,
When feeling down, I'll lift you to the extremes!

For it's you and only you that I breathe,
Love you all over, up top, underneath!

What must I do, say to convince,
'Cause, girl, I've loved you ever since!

If you'll simply give me one try,
Smile on your face, gleam in your eye

NO CHANGE

At times, loving you, somewhat frightening,
Major storm, that thunder and lightning.

Yet living on the edge, this path I chose,
You could be right, might be wrong, who knows?

Haven't changed, yea I still feel the same,
Pass that by me again, what's your name?

'Cause a name's not much, it's what's deep inside,
It's only you in whom I can confide.

Trying to say, my dream come true,
No, for real, if you only knew.

MEET GEORGE JETSON

I should have known, those days couldn't last,
Were too damn good, therefore, live the past.

If I could enter a time machine,
Return, go back, wouldn't that be keen?

Step in, close hatch behind, then it's blastoff,
Never come down, loving that upstairs loft!

All this time, thought I was a space cadet,
Ready for this, you ain't seen nothing yet!

For I'm an odyssey way out there in space,
Don't believe, then study the lines on my face.

Yea I've been around the block once or twice,
At times were hard, looking back it was nice!

Life on this planet, there's no guarantee,
Fly away with me, and you might just see!

KANDY

Synonymous to a locked door,
Little boy in your candy store.

It's like that of a delicious s'more,
Not giving in, makes me want you more.

Say you will come over to my side,
For it's you in whom I wish to confide!

Like puppy love, we could hold hands,
That's my story, my word, I'll stand!

You're so shy, I'll make you blush,
Thinking of you makes me rush!

So please won't you open that locked door,
The one to your heart that I adore!

QUEEN BEE MINE

Like eight days a week, I just gotta see you more,
Deep within your heart, be that key, unlocks your door.

I want you as my soulmate, you can be my clone,
Without you in my life, never make it alone!

Genie out the bottle, my every wish come true,
'Cause, darlin', you're my miracle, things that you do!

If I could see the future, deep within your eyes,
Treat you like a queen, with the Q capitalized!

The truth, whole truth, what I'm saying is no lie,
For you, sweetheart, I'd gladly lay down and die!

Can't you see, it's the way it's supposed to be,
Ain't too proud to beg, I'm down on bended knee!

CAPTIVE

Do I stop or go, straddling this fence?
Should I cease fire, or do I commence?

Got me so confused, don't know what to do,
Tell me so we both know, this much is true.

I'm under your spell, so captivated,
In a trance, more than infatuated!

I want you, I need you, what more must I say?
Need you tomorrow, hell, I need you today!

So here we go again, begging you please,
If necessary, will drop to my knees!

THIS MASK

If you don't wanna know, then don't ask,
Don't much prefer, removing this mask.

See, it's this mask that I've worn so long,
Hell and back keeps me singing this song.

So I'll keep singing till the cows come home,
Message in a bottle, I'm not alone!

Not alone either, don't back down,
They'll laugh at you, as if a clown.

But you're no clown outside or in,
I know your heart so deep within!

Unlike that mask, will deteriorate,
I'll accept you as you are, wipe your slate!

THE FIND

Running the roads, cool wind in my hair,
Looking for you, searching everywhere.

I've looked here, I've looked over there,
Must admit, starting to get scared.

Where else must I look, it's you I gotta find,
If not, I'll lose my ever-loving mind!

Once I find you, need to strongly inform,
That only you can stop this raging storm!

I've tried others, they just won't do,
'Cause wasn't until I found you!

YOUR SONG

Oftentimes, wish that I was a song,
I'd stay in your heart all your life long.

Be that special tune you frequently think of,
Deep in your soul, I'd warm fill you with love!

Take you on a journey, new horizon,
Over and over sing, never be done.

Never get old, like the first time you heard,
For you're my song, sweetheart, give you my word!

Yes, I wish, my dear, that I was a song,
I'd gladly sing for you all your life long!

UTMOST IMPORTANCE

Was of more importance, put off 'nother day,
'Stead of sitting down, saying what had to say.

Always more important, your things to do,
Yet now looking back, just wish that we knew.

For time spent together, then time spent apart,
Must realize, have only one life, one heart!

One day, our hearts and our lives will come to an end,
It's realization, must acknowledge, my friend!

Before then, I pray we get it right,
With the man upstairs basking in His light!

PREVALENT SIGNS

The world around us, just watch the news,
Won't take long till you're singing the blues.

No, really, we're not doing so well,
How do you still figure there's no hell?

The signs are out there, so prevalent,
A warning from above, heaven sent!

Still continue to live our selfish ways,
Gonna find out soon, one of these days.

Not until then, realize we weren't so great,
But then be a dollar short, a day too late!

DOCTOR'S ORDERS

Went to see the doctor just the other day,
He said I might not wanna hear what he has to say.

Son, something's not right with your liver,
The way it was said made me shiver!

All those years of hard living and strong juice,
Might as well go out, tie yourself a noose!

On the other hand, there's an alternative,
Up to you whether you want to die or live!

Told me of this man, many moons ago,
If caught a glimpse, I would never let go!

He still makes house calls, you must believe,
Any, every ailment, will relieve!

For He's the best doctor, He's got the cure,
Will prescribe something so cleansing and pure!

His name is Jesus, He's God in man's form,
Will help you ride out all of life's storms!

HAPPY BIRTHDAY TO YOU

Many moons ago, witnessed you come out,
Since then convinced, you're an angel, no doubt!

A twin sister, as beautiful as her,
You'll always feel that void, of this I'm sure!

Wish could wave a wand, take away your loss,
But I'm only human, I'm not the boss!

You're more than a daughter, you're such a dear friend,
You give unto others true love, girl, you send!

I'm so proud of you, I can't say enough,
Sorry, Daddun wasn't there all that much!

MY LOVE BUG

That time of year, the love bugs are out,
My love for you, don't you ever doubt.

Had me the first time, witnessed that smile,
Ever since then, captive all the while!

That scrumptious taste that dwells on my tongue,
Like the birds and bees, it's me you stung!

So now where do we go, tell where from here?
Please enlighten me, well, would you, my dear?

No need to fear, want that made clear,
For real, I'm the utmost sincere!

WAY BACK WHEN

Touched down in Cleveland, or was it Denver,
Tell the truth, I really don't remember.

It was sweet, best I can recall,
A wild stallion kicking the stall.

But we've tamed down now that we're older,
Know you reminisce, young and bolder.

Yet that's all right, gonna be okay,
Never forget, rompin' in the hay!

Looking back, if I could turn back time,
Better still, probably lose my mind.

NO TOMORROW

Gonna forget yesterdays, that's the past,
Wanna live for tomorrow, might just last.

Yet there's really no tomorrow, dare we think,
Sleep, awaken, tomorrow's today, in a blink.

When all's said and done, today's all we've got,
Would prefer a maybe 'stead of no, not.

I'm not your type, guess I have to agree,
So I plead the Fifth, Your Majesty.

Another court date, time for appeal,
Can lock me up, but I'll love you still!

OUTSIDE THE BOTTLE

Tend to find my dreams in the bottom of a bottle,
It' just that, well, this life is sometimes hard to swallow.

Then I saw you walking up those stairs,
Don't member much thereafter, who cares?

Poetry in motion, swaying east to west,
I'll forsake all the others, want the best!

Followed you up, only brought me way down,
Like a masquerade, the tears of a clown.

But that's okay, it was well worth the ride,
Deep within you, I found true love inside!

Climbing out of that bottle, step by step,
Still intoxicated inside your depths!

WOODSTOCK

Happy birthday to you, Woodstock,
My Lord, how the people did flock!

Half a mil, can you imagine?
Seems yesterday, yet way back then.

At a time of peace and war,
Looking back, haven't come too far!

Joe Cocker, Crosby, Stills, Nash, Young, then Jimi,
Blasting out those tunes, louder than a hemi!

Cars better built, the air was clean,
Back then, the atmosphere was serene!

Need to look within, make a hard change,
No seriously, let's rearrange!

What about that peace, just stop killing,
Make a comeback, gotta be willing!

IN THE AIR

It's in the atmosphere, you must know it's near,
Deep within, no denial, living the state of fear!

Can keep believing that nothing's changed,
We all know, have got to rearrange!

Come on, when younger, this easy life we chose,
Now getting older, world's coming to a close!

Refuse to lay down easy, lose this battle,
Can't see being caged, like a herd of cattle.

For they're captive, and forever they'll remain,
Personally, each morn, seek to remove my stains.

SITTER OF THE STARS

Keep it in place, sitter of the stars,
Through times of peace, then times of wars.

Makes the waves crash upon the sandy shores,
That's simply the least, can do so much more!

Can even change our stone-ridden hearts,
Don't believe, ask Him, give you a new start!

For that's why He came, His work is done,
Sent us His only begotten Son!

'Cause He's the sitter, keeper of the stars,
It's our job to answer Him when He calls!

DOG GONE

Once upon a time, there was this lad,
Looking back now, it seems so sad.

This girl of his dreams, she just wouldn't stay,
He had it all, but threw it all away!

His inner man, the struggles inside,
In her, he only wanted to confide.

Battle was over, said she was done,
All he ever wanted was to be one!

Couldn't have her, so he left for the coast,
Of a broken heart, he gave up the ghost.

GOD'S HUMOR

Think 'bout it, He's gotta have a sense of humor,
No, for real, this is fact, not merely rumor!

Why else on earth were we created?
His pure love, not infatuated!

You see there's something we must understand,
We were formed from dust, He's the boss, the man!

Don't believe this, seek the heaven's above,
He's the way, the truth, and the life. He is love!

Bowing heads tonight, praying tomorrow we'll be awoke,
Let's not forget, He's got a sense of humor, but it's no joke.

TESTING ZONE

Must remember, this is merely a test,
When trials are thrown our way, we must do our best!

For the clouds may thicken, both dark and gray,
Yet the sun will rise, bringing forth a new day!

'Cause this is nothing, don't let it get you down,
Tomorrow's a new day, soon be coming around!

This world will trample, give it their best shot,
Then stand up and ask, "Is that all you got?"

For we'll awaken, one day in eternity,
Then and only then, passing those test, set us free!

LEFT ME HANGING

If my love were a leaf, hanging from a tree,
Only wish you were there, hanging with me!

Never thought I'd find another quite like you,
It's simply the way you do the things you do!

Free to say things that are on my mind,
Another like you I'll never find!

Times I wonder if you truly feel the same,
Please tell me now, don't put me to shame.

Guess I'll close, don't have much more to say,
Miss, love you more, with each passing day!

MY BETTER PART

Probably tired, again apologize,
I'm tired too, finally realized.

How can I say I'm sorry in this song,
How do I make it right, knowing I'm wrong?

Without you, I just don't know where to start,
Before we met, swear didn't have much heart!

But now you're my better part
Sweet and sour, kinda tart!

Swear I'll love you all my life, then some,
You make my heart palpitate like a drum!

Lie if you must, say you'll stay with me for life,
Seriously though, would you please be my wife?

MUSIC

It's that low-down, soulful rift of strings,
That ecstasy only music brings.

If ever heard, you'll never forget,
'Nother love like this, you'll never get.

Telling you friends, by far she's the best,
Bring you up, then lay with, when need rest!

That sweet kiss so early in the morn,
Though night before, quite tattered and torn.

That gorgeous tune, that last note,
Gotta go, that's all she wrote!

WILD CARD

Got me higher than a Georgia pine,
Sweeter than any strawberry wine!

How high can you take me, what I wanna know,
Sure as I'm sitting here, I'm ready to go!

The cards are in your hands, you hold the deck,
You're making my life a physical wreck!

But wreck me if you wish, I like this game,
You dealt the cards, I'll never be the same!

'Cause even if I lose, I still win,
Go head, reshuffle, and let's play again!

KINGS OF KINGS

I awoke this morn, had dreamt I was a king,
Rubbed my eyes, felt no crown, throne, was same ole thing.

But that's okay. We're all kings and queens,
Don't lose faith in yourself, know what I mean?

All different for a purpose, yet all the same,
Never let anyone tell you, that you're lame!

Life can be deceiving, fill you with lies,
That's simply the devil, trying to disguise!

Because that's what he does, ain't nothing but sin,
Turn to the King of kings, in Jesus's name. Amen!

DREAM GIRL

Girl, it's you, why would I look for another?
'Cause you're in my world, there is no other.

Now I have a purpose to awaken,
You're like the reason, I'm not mistaken!

Abruptly awoken, midst of a gorgeous dream,
You and I were afloat, on a crystal blue stream!

Wanted so badly, to go back to sleep,
All I could do was grab tissue and weep.

See what you do. Damn it. It's just not fair,
For without you, my life's a mere nightmare!

DREAMS

Wanted to remind you. So this you'll know,
Always told you, you'll miss me when I go,

Living on borrowed time, never can tell,
I thought I'd be here forever, oh well.

Like I thought, you'd always be around,
There I went thinking, look what I found,

I found that dreams don't always come true,
Like the dream, I thought I found in you!

But to dream means I'd have to sleep,
Couldn't do that, I'm in too deep!

ENDLESS SAIL

This sail's grown weary, trying to reach shore,
Hands have grown tired, merely grasping the oars.

But I'll keep rowing all night long,
Wind and waves, continue to grow strong.

Strong is the battle, come what may,
I thank God it's a brand-new day!

I've got no time, no time to rest,
Have gotta strive, to do my best!

'Cause that's how I roll, it's what I do,
When all's said and done, I pray you knew!

ANOTHER DAY IN PARADISE

These buckets of rain that soak my pillow,
Fall from my eyes like a weeping willow.

Another lonely day spent without you,
There I went thinking, I thought you were true!

Wish you luck wherever you are,
I hope you find your shooting star!

Thought I'd found mine, but was I wrong,
Days are empty, nights are so long!

Guess I'll see you, not anymore,
Gotta go, need to mop the floor.

GRANTED TAKEN

Seems I tend to take, this life for granted,
Just that when I dream, feel so enchanted.

One of these days, might just get it right,
Maybe tomorrow, won't be tonight,

Still try and try as I may,
Never seems to work out my way!

But I'll keep fighting 'cause that's what I do,
Any suggestions, oh, I thought you knew,

There I go thinking, thinking once again,
Must have been an afterthought, that was back when!

DECISIONS, DECISIONS

Bombarded by decisions every day,
We must decide what to think, do, and say.

Making all these decisions bring much stress,
No wonder our lives are in such a mess!

Should I do this, do that, gotta decide,
That out-of-control, roller-coaster ride.

With each decision, face consequences,
Make up mind, no time to straddle fences!

Come down to it, it's up to you and I,
So what cha think about that, you decide.

HOPELESS ROMANTIC

Hopeless romantic, makes me a fanatic,
Hopeless dreams, could become an addict.

If I could only stop my mind, might just sleep,
Guess it's too late for that, I'm in too deep!

You're more than my lover, you're my best friend,
More than physical, it's from deep within!

Between the two, why must we make things so hard?
If I'm out of line again, please disregard!

So please don't stop, whatever it is you do,
'Cause old as I am, make me feel brand-new!

UNITY

Hypothetically speaking, you and I,
Like a dream come true, makes me wanna cry.

We're in this together, this I used to doubt,
Looking back, baby girl, what's it all about?

Searched this land from coast to coast,
Still comes back to you, being the most!

Seem to be on my ever-loving mind,
It's you for me, me for you, just my kind.

Looking back throughout this mess,
We'll find true togetherness!

SOMEDAY

My share of mistakes, life's imperfection,
Not crazy 'bout this part, 'bout this section.

'Cause wanna be perfect in an imperfect world,
So damn frustrating, it makes my head swirl!

There's only one that's perfect, knew this all along,
Like that fine-tuned melody, your number-one song.

Keep playing till my hands grow numb,
I know to some, this might sound dumb.

It's how I see it, so how I play,
I'll get back with you some other day!

VALLEY BELOW

All strive to be on that mountain up top,
Yet it's times, we just don't know when to stop.

Then there are times in the valley below,
You have to have been there, for this I know!

Gotta go through hell, get to heaven's sky,
Trying to discern, still ask myself why.

This valley I'm in, merely a test,
One day soon, in paradise I'll rest!

All will be forgotten, all will be past,
Forever on that mountain, my dire quest!

IN THE AIR

It's in the atmosphere, you must all know it's near,
Deep within, no denial, living in the state of fear!

Can keep believing that nothing's changed,
We all know, have got to rearrange!

Come on, when younger, this easy life we chose,
Now getting older, world's coming to a close.

Refuse to lay down easy, lose this battle,
Can't see being caged, like a herd of cattle.

For they're held captive, and forever they'll remain,
Personally, each morn, seek to remove my stains!

SHOW YOUR LOVE

Be careful, could be closer than we think,
This ship we call Earth, could be 'bout to sink!

There's prevalent signs out there, signs showing,
Could be a warning, yet still not knowing?

Maybe treat others, like wanna be treated ourself,
How about show some love, start taking Him off the shelf!

You never know, He might want recognition,
Was one reason, He sent one and only Son!

But look how we're carrying on down here,
Of Him, we show no reverential fear!

LACK OF BEHAVIOR

In spite of our best behavior,
We're still in need of a Savior!

His name is Jesus, the only one,
For our sake, at Calvary, got things done!

Our time and belief, we must invest,
I'm trying to tell you, He's the best!

And if you're still skeptic, yea still yet,
Cast your bet on Him, He's your best bet!

Troublesome times, we must endure,
He'll see us through, of this I'm sure!

REDEMPTION

I'll always remember, never forget You,
Knowing You'll, always, remember me too!

Long as I awake, long as I can dream,
I'll keep believing that You can redeem!

Knowing in You and You alone is life,
Our only refuge through mountains and strife!

Our shelter, our cover, while on this earth,
From before His conception, virgin birth!

There's hope in knowing, through all this turmoil,
Formed us from dust, we'll return to His soil.

PASSING THROUGH

Funny how sometimes, life gets in our way,
Gotta understand, we're not here to stay.

Merely passing through for a short while,
It's like running a race, make that mile.

'Cause it will be over before we know,
Really need to tell you before you go!

Tell you 'bout Jesus, there's power in His name,
If and when you meet Him, never be the same!

Look around, we're in a chaotic state,
Pray you come to Him before it's too late!

CLOSING PRAYER

Tumbleweed, was quite the rolling stone,
Looking back, find myself alone.

So alone, how could you do?
Never suspect, never knew.

Then again, be careful what you pray,
Could backfire, end up other way.

Don't let that stop you from praying more,
'Cause in due time, He'll bless still more!

It's in the air, we're coming to a close,
Hey, could be tomorrow, God only knows!

THE END

I'm lonely too, girl, just like all the rest,
Still seeking salvation, indeed my quest!

Remain searching until then just might find,
If not, might just lose my ever-loving mind.

Searching all this time, sure takes its toll,
Hungry, thirsty, won't You feed my soul?

I'm still out here, Lord, seems like forever,
Learned along the way, never say never.

Fed my soul with the gift of salvation,
Freely given, Your only begotten Son!

These days, might just be living the end,
Can't we live in harmony, my friend?

ACKNOWLEDGMENTS

At this time, I'd like to sincerely thank those close to me who helped me with the tools and/or inspiration that were required toward the making of this book.

I wish to thank both my sister, Nanette, and my daughter, Crystal, who were more help than they could possibly imagine!

And last but certainly not least, I want to thank our heavenly Father, Lord God Almighty, for blessing me with this gift of writing! My prayer is that it reaches others for His glory!

PS: Thanks to all my readers; if not for you, this wouldn't have been possible! Can't forget to thank my earthly father, who passed this year. He was and will always remain unforgettable! Let's just say, he did it "His Way!" Thankful to him also. For the legacy of writing he left me!!! Love and miss you Dad!!!

P.S.S: Can't forget to thank my earthly father, who passed this year. He was and will always remain unforgettable! Let's just say, he did it "His Way!" Thankful to him also. For the legacy of writing he left me!!! Love and miss you Dad!!!

ABOUT THE AUTHOR

James Gomez Jr. was born and raised in southern Louisiana and resides there still. He had two sets of twins, of which three children remain, one of whom was lost at a young age due to SIDS! This book goes out to them: Rachel, Crystal, Bryan, and Brittany.